Backyard Animals
Mosquitoes

Christine Webster

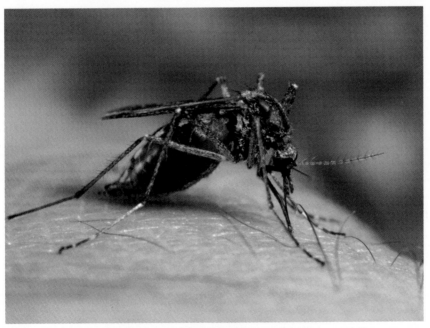

Weigl Publishers Inc.

Published by Weigl Publishers Inc.
350 5th Avenue, Suite 3304, PMB 6G
New York, NY 10118-0069
Website: www.weigl.com

Library of Congress Cataloging-in-Publication Data

Webster, Christine.
 Mosquitoes / Christine Webster.
    p. cm. -- (Backyard animals)
 Includes index.
 ISBN 978-1-60596-086-9 (hard cover : alk. paper) -- ISBN 978-1-60596-087-6 (soft
cover : alk. paper)
 1. Mosquitoes--Juvenile literature. I. Title.
 QL536.W427 2010
 595.77'2--dc22

                                    2009004447

Printed in China
1 2 3 4 5 6 7 8 9 0 13 12 11 10 09

Editor Heather C. Hudak
Design Terry Paulhus

All of the Internet URLs given in the book were valid at the time of publication.
However, due to the dynamic nature of the Internet, some addresses may have
changed, or sites may have ceased to exist since publication. While the author
and publisher regret any inconvenience this may cause readers, no responsibility
for any such changes can be accepted by either the author or the publisher.

Photo Credits

Every reasonable effort has been made to trace ownership and to obtain
permission to reprint copyright material. The publishers would be pleased
to have any errors or omissions brought to their attention so that they may
be corrected in subsequent printings.

Weigl acknowledges Getty Images as its primary photo supplier for this title.

Contents

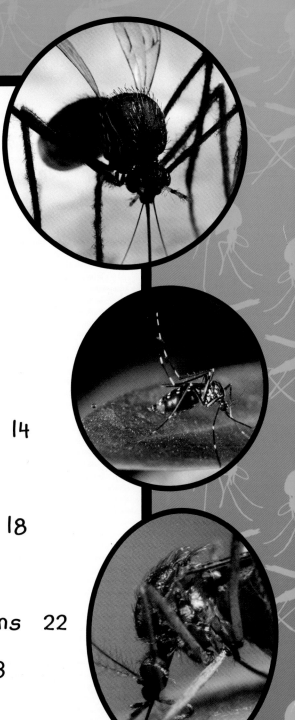

Meet the Mosquito

Mosquitoes are flying insects. They have narrow bodies with long thin legs. Mosquitoes are about 0.25 to 0.5 inches (0.6 to 1.3 centimeters) in length.

Although tiny, most people think mosquitoes are pests. They need blood to make eggs. To get the blood, mosquitoes bite people and animals.

Mosquitoes are found all over the world. They live in lowland areas and high above mountains. Mosquitoes are even found in very cold places, such as the Arctic.

Mosquitoes can smell people and animals from up to 100 feet (30 meters) away.

Hundreds of thousands of mosquitoes are born around the world each day.

All about Mosquitoes

There are more than 2,700 mosquito **species**. New mosquito species are found all the time. About 150 species live in North America. Here, most mosquitoes belong to one of three main groups. These are *Aedes*, *Anopheles*, and *Culex*.

Mosquitoes are an important part of the web of life. This is because many animals eat mosquitoes. Dragonflies, frogs, bats, birds, and fish often **prey** on mosquitoes. If mosquitoes were to disappear from Earth, animals that eat them may not have enough food.

Mosquitoes weigh between 0.00009 and 0.0004 of an ounce (2.6 and 11.3 milligrams).

Types of Mosquitoes

Aedes

- Lays its eggs in **floodwaters**
- Includes the Asian tiger and yellow-fever mosquitoes

Anopheles

- Most often breeds in permanent fresh waters, such as rivers
- Includes the common **malaria** mosquito

Culex

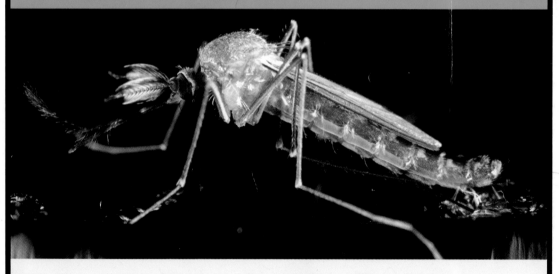

- Breeds in still water that does not flow, such as puddles or ponds
- Includes the northern house mosquito

Mosquito History

Mosquitoes have been on Earth for millions of years. In 300 B.C., **Aristotle** made notes about the life cycle of mosquitoes. He called these insects *emphis*. The word *mosquito* has been in use since 1583. It is Spanish for "little fly."

In the early 1900s, people learned that some mosquitoes carry infections and disease. These include **yellow fever** and malaria. Asian tiger mosquitoes have been in the United States since 1985. They can carry **encephalitis** and **dengue fever**.

In 1999, the **West Nile virus** was brought to the United States by mosquitoes. Today, this disease is found all over North America.

Mosquitoes were once three times as large as their current size.

In North America, it is rare for a human to get a disease from a mosquito.

Mosquito Shelter

Mosquitoes are always active in warm parts of the world. In other places, they may hibernate for the winter. During this time, they may live in human houses, animal burrows, or logs.

All mosquitoes make their homes near water. This is because they lay their eggs is still or slow-moving water. Shallow pools of rainwater, ponds, and lakes can be a breeding ground for mosquitoes.

Adult mosquitoes do not live in water. However, they rarely travel more than one mile (1.6 km) from the place where they hatched. They prefer to live in dark places, such as trees, weeds, and long grasses.

Large numbers of mosquito larvae, or baby mosquitoes, can live in a small bottle of water.

Mosquitoes can fly at speeds of about 1 to 1.5 miles (1.6 to 2.4 kilometers) per hour.

Mosquito Features

Like all insects, mosquitoes have three basic body parts. These are the head, thorax, and abdomen. Mosquitoes also have many special features to help them live in nature.

HEAD

Mosquitoes have **sensors** on their head. They use their sensors to find prey. These sensors also sense heat, movement, and odor. **Antennae** are one type of sensor. The antennae of a female mosquito have short **whorls** of hair. The male antennae are long and bushy.

MOUTH

A female mosquito has a long mouth. It looks like a little piece of thread. A mosquito's mouth is called the proboscis. The proboscis is used to pierce the skin of prey and inject **saliva**. It is also used to suck blood and to feed.

WINGS

A mosquito has a pair of long, thin wings. Small scales cover the wings. Mosquitoes can flap their wings about 300 times per second. This makes a buzzing sound.

THORAX

The thorax is the part of the body between the neck and the abdomen. Mosquitoes have a narrow thorax. The wings and legs attach to the thorax.

LEGS

Mosquitoes have six long legs.

What Do Mosquitoes Eat?

Only female mosquitoes feed on blood. They need blood to produce eggs. Females search for food during the early mornings and evenings. Though they often bite people, they prefer to get blood from animals, such as horses, cattle, and birds. Females need a new blood meal each time they lay eggs.

Both male and female mosquitoes get juices and nectar from plants and flowers. Larvae eat tiny plant and animal matter found in the water.

Female mosquitoes will feed from many animals, including birds, fish, snakes, lizards, frogs, and toads.

Some female mosquitoes can drink about two-and-a-half times their own weight in blood.

Mosquito Life Cycle

Three to five days after a mosquito forms, it is ready to mate. Once a female mates, she looks for a blood meal to help form her eggs. Then, she will lay the eggs. Female mosquitoes can lay between 1,000 and 3,000 eggs in their lifetime.

Eggs

Females often lay eggs at night. They may lay eggs every third night for their entire life. Eggs are laid one at a time or in a group. A group of eggs is called a mosquito egg raft. It is made up of about 40 to 400 tiny white eggs.

Larvae

Two to three days later, the eggs hatch into larvae, or wrigglers. Larvae live at the surface of the water. They breathe through air tubes that poke above the water. This tube is called a siphon. Larvae shed their skin many times as they grow. They eat bits of **organic** matter. Larvae can swim and dive if they are disturbed.

The life cycle of a mosquito lasts only a few weeks. There are four stages. These are egg, larva, pupa, and adult. An adult male mosquito only lives for about a week. A female lives from a few weeks to one month.

Pupae

Larvae molt four times before they turn into pupae. This takes two to three days. Pupae live just below the surface of the water. They breathe through tubes and do not eat. Pupae enclose themselves in a case that is like a **cocoon**.

Adults

After a few days, the pupa's skin splits open. The adult comes mosquito out. Adult mosquitoes will hide in a safe area until their body parts harden. Then, they will fly away to find food and search for a mate.

Encountering Mosquitoes

Most times, if a female mosquito lands on you, she will bite. She does this by sticking the long, skinny part of her mouth into the skin. The mosquito's saliva enters the skin. The saliva has a special substance that keeps the blood around the bite flowing freely. This allows the mosquito to suck blood easily. The saliva stays inside your skin, making the bite spot itchy.

There are many ways to avoid mosquito bites. When you are outdoors, keep your skin covered. Wear pants and long-sleeved shirts if you are playing in tall grasses and bushes. Mosquitoes like the smell of perfume, soap, and shampoo. Try not to use these items. Stay away from still water where mosquitoes lay their eggs.

Useful Websites

To learn more about mosquitoes, check out **www.mosquito.org**.

Mosquitoes prefer dark colors. They are more likely to stay away from people wearing light colors.

Myths and Legends

There are many myths and legends about mosquitoes. A Vietnamese legend tells how a man brought his wife back to life with three drops of his own

blood. Later, the woman wanted to leave him, and the man asked for his blood back. She cut her finger to give him the blood, but she died. The woman returned to life as a mosquito. She buzzed after her husband, trying to get the blood that would bring her back to life.

An African legend tells how a mosquito lied to an iguana. The iguana became upset and frightened another animal. Other animals became upset as a result. Over time, they learned that the mosquito was to blame. Today, he buzzes in people's ears to find out if the animals are still angry.

Ancient Mayans believed that mosquitoes were spies. As they sucked a person's blood, they would learn that person's name and other details.

The Great Father Mosquito

This is a Tuscarora Indian legend about a mosquito.

Once upon a time, there lived a giant mosquito. When he flew through the air, the Sun was hidden, and day turned to night. When the mosquito was hungry, he would carry people away. Everyone feared the giant mosquito. Warriors tried to destroy it, but they could not. The warriors called a meeting. Together, they prayed to the Creator to help them destroy the mosquito.

Bat and Spider heard the warriors' cries for help. Bat flew into the sky to battle the mosquito. Spider spun a large web to try to catch the mosquito. The mosquito flew away, but Bat chased him. Mosquito flew into the Spider's huge web. The mosquito was destroyed, but tiny mosquitoes were born from his blood. They had sharp stingers and attacked everyone. To this day, thousands of mosquitoes roam Earth. Bat hunts them every night, and spider spins a web to catch them.

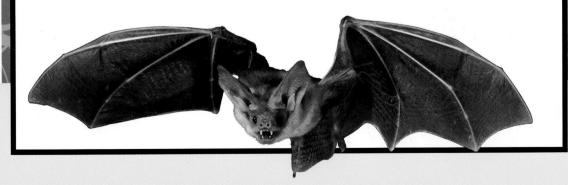

Frequently Asked Questions

Do other animals hunt mosquitoes?

Answer: Mosquitoes have many **predators**. Fish, dragonflies, birds, bats, and frogs are just some of the animals that eat mosquitoes.

How can I keep mosquitoes out of my yard?

Answer: The best way to keep mosquitoes out of your yard is to destroy places where they can breed. Begin by dumping water that pools in old tires or containers. Be sure to clean barrels, plant pots, swimming pools, gutters, and birdbaths often.

Do other insects look like mosquitoes?

Answer: Many other insects look like mosquitoes. These include crane flies, midges, mayflies, dance flies, and wood gnats.

Puzzler

See if you can answer these questions
about mosquitoes.

1. What do male mosquitoes eat?
2. How fast can mosquitoes flap their wings?
3. Where do mosquitoes lay their eggs?
4. What are the stages of the mosquito's life cycle?
5. What causes a mosquito bite to itch?

Answers: 1. nectar and juices from flowers and plants 2. 250 times per second 3. in water 4. eggs, larvae, pupae, adults 5. saliva left under the skin

Find Out More

There are many more interesting things to learn about mosquitoes. Look for these books at your library so you can learn more.

Markle, Sandra. *Mosquitoes: Tiny Insect Troublemakers*. Lerner Publications, 2007.

Piehl, Janet. *Flying Mosquitoes*. First Avenue Editions, 2006.

Words to Know

antennae: long, thin body parts that extend from an insect's head

Aristotle: an important Greek scientist and philosopher, or thinker, from ancient times

cocoon: a protective coil of silk

dengue fever: a disease spread by the bite of an infected *Aedes* mosquito

encephalitis: swelling of the brain

floodwaters: the water that overflows as a result of a flood

malaria: a disease that causes chills, fever, and sweating

organic: living tissue from plants, animals, and fungus

predators: animals that hunt other animals for food

prey: to hunt another animal for food

saliva: watery liquid made in the mouth

sensors: body parts that receive and respond to signals

species: a group of animals or plants that have many features in common

West Nile virus: a disease that causes flulike symptoms that can be deadly

whorls: coils or spirals

yellow fever: a disease found in tropical countries that harms the liver and kidneys

Index